Shelter Dogs

Amazing Stories of Adopted Strays

Peg Kehret

PHOTOGRAPHS BY GREG FARRAR

ALBERT WHITMAN & COMPANY

MORTON GROVE, ILLINOIS

For Emilie Jacobson:
*A writer's best friends are a good dog
and a good agent.*

Also by Peg Kehret:
*Small Steps: The Year I Got Polio
Five Pages a Day: A Writer's Journey*

Library of Congress Cataloging-in-Publication Data

Kehret, Peg.
Shelter dogs: amazing stories of adopted strays / by Peg Kehret.
p. cm.
Summary: Tells the stories of eight stray dogs that were adopted from an animal
shelter and went on to become service dogs, actors, and heroes.
ISBN 10: 0-8075-7334-5 ISBN 13: 978-0-8075-7334-1 (hardcover)
ISBN 10: 0-8075-7336-1   ISBN 13: 978-0-8075-7336-5 (paperback)
1. Dogs—United States—Anecdotes—Juvenile literature.
2. Dog adoption—United States—Anecdotes—Juvenile literature.
3. Animal shelters—United States—Anecdotes—Juvenile literature.
[1. Dog adoption. 2. Animal shelters.] I. Title.
SF426.5.K438 1999 636.7—dc21 98-34760
CIP
AC

The design is by Scott Piehl.

For more information about Albert Whitman & Company,
please visit our web site at www.albertwhitman.com.

Acknowledgments

Although this book is about eight dogs, it could not have been written without the help of the people who live with those dogs. My heartfelt thanks to Megan Stanfel, Anne Gordon, Nita Baker, Helen Hughes, Susan Duncan, Jessica Mitchell, Ann Graves, Donna Amos, Taj Brumleve, and Cliff and Carol Chartrand for the time spent on interviews, photo sessions, follow-up phone calls, and e-mail. There's no doubt—dog lovers are the best people.

I also thank Nancy Buckingham McKenney, director of the Humane Society of Seattle/King County, for her encouragement at the start of this project and for suggesting dogs who might fit my criteria. Thanks, too, to Carla McAllister and Jody McInturff who also told me about special dogs.

Steve Gengo of the Redmond, Washington, Fire Department and Jeanne Hampl of the Prison Pet Partnership Program promptly returned calls and patiently answered questions. Margie Mitchell welcomed me to her home and kept me informed of her daughter's 4-H dog events. I am grateful for their help.

Thanks to Bill Larson, DVM, for sharing his memories of Kirby and to Andrea Wall for telling me about Bridgette's foster care.

Special thanks to Greg Farrar for his beautiful photographs and for his many years as a volunteer helping shelter dogs.

Contents

Introduction

Shelter dogs are dogs who have been turned in to an animal shelter. They are given away by their owners for a variety of reasons. Sometimes an owner "doesn't have enough time" for the dog or is moving to a place where dogs are not allowed. Some people let their dogs have puppies and then take the puppies to a shelter. People sometimes develop allergies to animals or get too sick to care for a dog.

Some shelters are run by a city or county government. Other shelters are private organizations, run by compassionate people who do their best to provide food, medical care, and attention to the animals while trying to find them permanent, loving homes.

Most of the dogs in this book came from the Humane Society for Seattle/King County, a nonprofit shelter in Washington State that also takes in cats, rabbits, birds, and other small animals. I have adopted two dogs and two cats from this shelter, and I do volunteer work there. The staff and the volunteers truly love the animals entrusted to them and work tirelessly to provide the best possible care for these homeless creatures. Animals are kept as long as there is space available and they remain adoptable. Sadly, some are eventually euthanized. Donations and service fees are this agency's only source of funds.

The motto of this facility is "Providing Love and Preventing Cruelty," and the workers there do both. When I say "the Humane Society" as I tell the stories of these special dogs, I am referring to this particular shelter.

But the truth is, there are many fine animal shelters, and all of them have wonderful animals available for adoption. There are hundreds of shelter dogs with every bit as much potential as the ones described in this book. All these dogs need are people to love them and give them homes.

Zorro

THE CHAMPION THAT NOBODY WANTED

Zorro leaps over a course of hurdles during a Flyball demonstration given by the Puget Sound Flyers at Volunteer Park in Seattle.

1

ZORRO, A GREAT DANE/mixed breed dog, was eight weeks old when he first came to the Humane Society. His original owner "couldn't find homes for all the puppies."

Like most puppies, Zorro was lively and lovable. Unlike most puppies, he had kennel cough and had to be confined to the medical ward until he recovered and could be put up for adoption.

Jet black, with white paws, chest, and throat and a bit of white at the tip of his tail, Zorro was a long-legged beauty. As he lost his cute puppy look, it was clear to even the most inexperienced dog person that he was going to be a mighty big dog. He had huge paws and soon weighed forty pounds.

When he recovered, he was moved to the adoption building, which has individual kennels down both sides of a wide walkway. Whenever visitors arrived, Zorro leaped eagerly against the front of the wire kennel, his long tail waving wildly. Nobody wanted to adopt such a big and rowdy dog.

Weeks went by, Zorro grew and grew, and no one chose him. Finally, when he had been at the shelter for three months, he was adopted by a family who said they wanted a big dog and were prepared to give him the care he needed. Zorro galloped away from the kennel, tugging on his leash, his tail flapping like a windshield wiper.

His happiness did not last long. Seven months later, the family returned him to the Humane Society. They said they didn't have time to exercise him, so they kept him shut in the house. Bored and restless, Zorro had begun to chew on the furniture. The family did not want a destructive dog.

By then, Zorro weighed seventy pounds, and his head reached the countertop at the adoption center. His energy level matched his size, and since he had never been taught any manners, he was now extremely hard to handle.

Of course, no one knows for sure what went through Zorro's mind as he was brought back to the Humane Society where he had already spent so much time. But he must have wondered why he was again left alone in a kennel.

Each dog who awaits adoption at the Humane Society has paperwork attached to the kennel telling his history. Every attempt is made to be honest about any problems. For example, the history might say "Does not get along with cats" or "Needs continuing treatment for ear mites." This information helps potential adopters as they try to choose a dog that will fit their lifestyle.

Now that Zorro was in the shelter a second time, his paperwork showed that he was a "returned" dog who had not worked out with his first adopting family. The paperwork also said that Zorro did not know how to obey and was known to chew—problems that would need to be corrected.

At the age of one year, Zorro, through no fault of his own, had four strikes against him: his size, his history of a failed adoption, his lack of training, and his chewing. Still, the staff hoped that some loving person would give Zorro a second chance.

Weeks passed.

No one took Zorro.

That summer, the Humane Society put on a three-week day camp for youth from troubled families. During the camp, volunteer coaches helped these young people take shelter dogs through a dog obedience class.

A Seattle woman, Megan Stanfel, offered to be a coach. Her group of campers chose to work with Zorro.

Every day for three weeks, Megan's young helpers exercised Zorro and cleaned up after him. They groomed him, brushing his black coat until it shone. They taught him to sit and stay. They decorated a special collar for him.

Zorro thrived under this attention, and he learned each lesson quickly. He no longer jumped on visitors. He knew how to walk properly on a leash.

Although Zorro was the largest dog in camp, he was never aggressive toward the other dogs or to any of the people in the program. The campers nicknamed him "the Gentle Giant."

Megan and her young workers knew that they were helping Zorro become more adoptable. They groomed him especially well on Fridays so that he would look his best over the weekend, when most adoptions take place. Despite their efforts, Zorro stayed at the shelter.

On the final day of camp, the dogs "graduated."

Zorro wore his new collar and marched in to the music "Pomp and Circumstance." The camp's obedience trainers voted him "Most Cooperative Dog."

News photographers attended the graduation, and Megan urged them to photograph Zorro. She hoped someone would see his picture and fall in love with this handsome animal whose good manners now matched his good looks. But the photographers said black dogs are harder to photograph than light-colored ones; once again, Zorro was not selected.

Megan attached a note to the paperwork on Zorro's kennel, saying how well he had worked with children during the summer camp and how quickly he had learned his obedience lessons. She mentioned that he was voted Most Cooperative Dog and that he got along with all the other dogs in camp.

Although the camp was over, Megan continued to volunteer at the Humane Society. Each time she came, she went first to Zorro's kennel, hoping he would not be there. He always was.

One day Megan gave him a bath so he would look and smell his best. But a month went by, and still Zorro had no family.

Each year, the Humane Society's main fund-raiser is

an event called "Tuxes and Tails." This consists of an auction and a celebrity/pet fashion show where sports stars, radio and television personalities, and other celebrities model the latest fashions. As the celebrities walk down the runway, each is accompanied by a dog. Some bring their own dogs; most use dogs from the shelter.

Tuxes and Tails always gets wide media coverage, so Megan arranged for Zorro to be in the show. Maybe someone in the audience or watching news clips on TV would want to adopt him. She practiced walking with him, helping him remember how to act on a leash.

The celebrity wore a black tuxedo; Zorro wore a crisp white bow tie—plus his usual black fur coat and white bib. Zorro pranced down the runway, tail wagging. The audience applauded loudly for the handsome pair—but nobody asked to adopt Zorro.

Megan and her husband, Ken, discussed adopting Zorro themselves. They already had two dogs. Buddy, a mix of German shepherd, Lab, and husky, had a seizure disorder and needed special medical care. Lester, a beagle/basset mix, had been abused before Megan and Ken found him abandoned in a park, and he was still fearful of new situations.

Megan and Ken worried that bringing a huge, rambunctious dog like Zorro into their home would not be fair to Buddy and Lester. They weren't sure it would be fair to Zorro, either.

"Zorro is so special," Megan told Ken. "He deserves to be the only dog in a loving family—not the third dog."

Megan often cried with frustration when she arrived at the shelter and found Zorro still there. She always took him to the outdoor courtyard for exercise. Other volunteers exercised him, too, but these brief encounters were not enough for such a large and lively dog.

As weeks became months and Zorro remained in the kennel, he slipped back into his old habits. Without regular practice, he forgot the obedience lessons he had learned. Zorro became hard to handle again.

As the days slid past, Zorro gradually withdrew. He was always glad to see Megan, but other volunteers could no longer coax him out of the kennel. Zorro was quickly becoming unadoptable. If he quit interacting with people, he would have to be euthanized.

Finally Megan could not stand to watch Zorro deteriorate any longer. She and Ken agreed to give Zorro the only chance he would get; they adopted him themselves.

While Ken drove, Megan sat in the back seat with Zorro. All the way home, he licked her hands as his tail beat against the car window. Happy sounds bubbled from his throat, and he physically shook with joy.

"I promise you," Megan told him, "that you will never, ever go back to the Humane Society."

At home, Buddy and Lester met the newcomer. They sniffed Zorro, and Zorro sniffed them. Tails wagged. Low-slung Lester walked under Zorro and stood there; when Zorro jumped out of the way, Lester walked under him again. Buddy sat down to watch. It quickly became a game, and both dogs seemed happy to have a new playmate.

When Megan and Ken took Zorro inside, he calmly followed them through the house, carefully keeping his tail under control.

"Zorro was absolutely no trouble," Megan says. "We expected it to be a huge adjustment for all of us. Instead, he fit right in. Although his head reaches the kitchen counter, he has never tried to take food. He is gentle with Lester and Buddy, and he loves his daily walks in the park."

Megan enrolled Zorro in a novice obedience class. He did so well that she continued with an advanced class.

One day the obedience instructor invited Megan and Zorro to attend a Flyball competition.

"A what?" Megan said.

"Flyball. It's a dog relay race. There are two teams of four dogs each. When the starter says 'Go!' the lead dog on each team races down a lane, jumping across four hurdles, and triggers a ball box with his paw. That releases a tennis ball. The dog catches the ball, makes a quick U-turn, and carries the ball back over the hurdles to the starting line. As soon as he gives the ball to his handler, the second dog on the team starts off. The race keeps going until all four dogs are finished. The team that's fastest wins."

Curious, Megan went to watch a Flyball race. She saw dogs of all sizes and breeds, including mixed breeds like Zorro, playing Flyball. The dogs and the people all seemed to be having fun. The dogs waited eagerly for their turns, some of them barking with excited anticipation.

Thinking that Flyball would provide good exercise for Zorro, Megan taught him the Flyball routine. He loved running fast and going over the jumps. He quickly caught on how to release the tennis ball from the box, and he always raced back to Megan with it, eager to get her approval and a treat. Before long, he did so well that he was invited to compete.

Right from the start, Zorro was good at Flyball. Soon he won a Flyball title and then another and then a third. He won ribbons and medals.

He was asked to join the Puget Sound Flyers, a Flyball demonstration team whose purpose is entertainment rather than racing. Zorro's team performs at half-time during many sporting events.

Megan took him to do shows at the University of Washington during basketball and soccer games. They traveled to Vancouver, British Columbia, in Canada, where they were the special guests of the Vancouver Grizzlies, a National Basketball Association team.

Zorro was classified as an "entertainer" as he crossed the border into Canada. After the Flyball performance, the Grizzlies provided Megan and Zorro with their own hotel suite for the night. It was definitely more luxurious than a kennel at the Humane Society!

"People tell me how lucky Zorro is that I adopted him," Megan says. "But I am the lucky one. He has enriched my life in so many ways."

Megan used to take the bus to the Humane Society because she didn't drive. After Zorro began Flyball competitions, Megan learned to drive and got her own car so that she could transport Zorro to his meets.

The obedience instructor who taught Zorro's classes saw the expert way Megan handled this large dog and offered her a part-time job. Megan now teaches obedience classes. Zorro sometimes goes along to demonstrate the proper methods. Zorro also took the necessary training to qualify as a therapy dog so Megan can take him to visit hospitalized children. Even the sickest children smile when they pet big, friendly Zorro.

Zorro's Flyball team was invited to provide the half-time entertainment at a Seattle Sonics basketball game. Each dog on the Puget Sound Flyers wore a new auburn-and-gold coat. With his black fur and golden eyes, Zorro looked particularly handsome.

The Key Arena in Seattle, where the Sonics play, was sold out that night, and when Zorro finished his routine, the crowd gave him a standing ovation.

As the applause echoed from the rafters, Megan stood with tears in her eyes. She thought of all the lonely months Zorro spent in the Humane Society shelter—months when no one wanted him.

Since then, Zorro has demonstrated Flyball at a New Jersey Nets game at the Meadowlands in East Brunswick, New Jersey; at a Cavaliers game in Cleveland, Ohio; and at New York Knicks games in Madison Square Garden in New York City. His team donates any profits from performance fees to animal welfare organizations or uses the money to buy new equipment and coats for the dogs. The team also does many free shows for charities, senior centers, and the University of Washington.

Whether it's a small group or a crowd of thousands, the response is always the same: everyone cheers for Zorro, the shelter dog who became a champion.

About Kennel Cough

Kennel cough is caused by a highly contagious virus that can be prevented by vaccination. A dog with kennel cough has a dry, raspy cough and may need a cough suppressant, anti-inflammatory drugs, or antibiotics. If untreated, kennel cough can lead to pneumonia. If you suspect your dog has kennel cough, take her to a veterinarian and keep her away from other dogs until she is well.

About Flyball

Flyball began in California in the early 1970s. Herbert Wagner made the first Flyball box that launched tennis balls and used it in his dog obedience classes as a fun activity for the dogs. When he demonstrated his new game on *The Tonight Show*, interest in Flyball spread quickly.

The North American Flyball Association, Inc. (NAFA) was formed in 1985 and adopted specific rules for Flyball competitions. For example, the jump heights must be set at four inches below the shoulders of the shortest dog competing, with the lowest hurdle eight inches. So the jumps for one team might not be the same height as the jumps of the opposing team. It all depends on the sizes of the dogs who are running. For this reason, most teams like to include at least one short dog.

Tracker

MOVIE-STAR DOG

Professional animal trainer Anne Gordon works with her movie-star dog, Tracker, who stands on his "mark" for lights, camera, and action at Anne's ranch outside Duvall, Washington.

2

～

*T*RACKER BEGAN LIFE as an unwanted puppy. Along with his eleven brothers and sisters, he was left at the Humane Society before he was old enough to be separated from his mother.

When this happens, the Humane Society places the puppies in foster homes with volunteers who will give them the extra care and attention (often including middle-of-the-night feedings) that such young animals need. The volunteers take the place of the mother dog.

Animals who go to foster homes as babies are often especially loving and gentle as adults. Because they receive lots of affection and tender care at an early age, they give great love in return. Pups who are left alone and not handled regularly do not learn to enjoy human companionship.

Tracker is a mixed-breed dog—probably part collie and perhaps part German shepherd or Akita. Perhaps. It's hard to tell for sure, and the people who brought the puppies in did not know or care. Tracker has a face like a collie's, with a long snout and expressive eyes. He has smooth white fur with a few large brown spots. A long, waving tail and one ear that flops over at the tip give him a distinctive look.

Whatever his breed, he got along well in foster care, and when he was old enough to be adopted, he was returned to the Humane Society. That's where he was at the age of eight weeks when Anne Gordon found him.

Anne is an animal trainer. With a college degree in biology and a minor in animal behavior, plus three years' experience as a zookeeper at Seattle's Woodland Park Zoo, Anne started her own company: Anne's Animal Actors. She trains wild and domestic animals of all kinds and prepares them to act in television shows, commercial productions, and movies. They also model for magazine and newspaper ads.

By the time she found Tracker, Anne was well known and highly sought after. Her credits included the movies *Homeward Bound, Free Willie 2, The Good*

Son, Home for the Holidays, and the television series *Rescue 911.*

Anne did not need another dog, but when she saw Tracker she was so taken by his good looks and eager-to-please personality that she decided to give him a home.

Anne had adopted other dogs and cats from the Seattle/King County Humane Society. She had also adopted animals from the Portland, Oregon, Humane Society and from the shelters of other animal welfare agencies. All became part of her business and members of her family.

Tracker went to Anne's home, deep in the woods in northern Washington State, where her other animal actors also live. Home for Anne Gordon and her four-legged friends is not merely a house. It is wooded acreage where each animal's needs are met.

Four wolves live in a half-acre of fenced forest. A pair of beavers, one male and one female, have side-by-side pens, each complete with its own swimming tub. When Anne bought these beavers from a fur farm, she saved their lives.

Two red foxes run to the fence to greet Anne whenever they see her coming. A pair of mule deer, veteran actors with many credits, have an entire fenced acre of woods all to themselves. Two raccoons, who were found orphaned as babies, amble about in their special enclosure.

The dog kennel contains a variety of mixed-breed dogs, each with its own spacious run and snug doghouse. When Anne walks to the kennel, every dog rushes to lick her hand. Each gets a turn to be out of the kennel every day, galloping around Anne's property. And they receive ongoing training to keep their acting skills sharp. Anne's assistants help care for and train the animals, and they take over for Anne when she is away.

At first Tracker lived inside Anne's house so she could bond with him and socialize him. The raccoons were babies then, and Tracker happily tolerated them as they climbed on his back and tried to play with his tail. This interaction was important because an animal actor must be able to get along with other animals of all kinds.

Anne began working with Tracker every day, teaching him all the basic obedience commands such as sit and stay. All of Anne's training is done with hand signals rather than voice commands so that she can direct her animals while they are being filmed.

When Tracker had mastered basic obedience, he began to accompany Anne when she took other animals on location. He watched while other dogs acted in films or got their pictures taken for magazines.

By going along at a young age, Tracker got used to the bright lights and noise and people. He learned to pay attention only to Anne's commands and not be distracted by anything else that was going on around him.

Tracker proved to be a quick learner who loved to go to work with Anne. Soon he auditioned for his own first part and got it.

Tracker's first acting job was in a television commercial for the Oregon State Lottery. Anne drove him to Portland, where the commercial was filmed. Tracker's part was not difficult: he had to lie on the floor with his head down, next to a woman in a chair. Then, when Anne gave the signal, Tracker was supposed to lift his head and perk up his ears as if something exciting had happened.

Tracker performed flawlessly. Anne knew he was a fine actor. She continued to teach him new commands and included agility training in his lessons.

In agility training, Tracker learned to go through tunnels, climb ladders, walk on elevated walks, and do a variety of jumps. Agility training is good for film work because it gives a dog confidence. Tracker seemed to like practicing these new skills.

A few months after Tracker made the lottery commercial, a movie producer contacted Anne. His company, The Edge Productions, planned to make a feature film based on the book *Summer of the Monkeys* by Wilson Rawles. There was a major role for a dog.

Whenever Anne is asked to provide animal actors, she first figures out exactly what the animal will be required to do. She reads the script and has the director fax her storyboards that spell out specific behavior for each scene. She also talks to the director by phone, to be certain there is no misunderstanding.

After Anne read *Summer of the Monkeys*, she knew that several of her dogs had the skills to play the part of the hound dog in the movie. Although the dog's role was important, it did not require doing any unusual or sophisticated tricks.

She sent the movie's director photos of the dogs who she felt could handle the role. She included Tracker. After seeing the photos, the director wanted to watch the dogs in action, so Anne made a video and sent that.

The director liked Tracker's unusual looks and the natural way he acted on screen. The decision was made: Tracker had his first part in a movie! He was two years old.

Four chimpanzees were also scheduled to work in this movie, so the first step was to make sure Tracker would get along with them. Although he was used to a wide variety of animals at Anne's house, he had never seen a chimpanzee.

Tracker and Anne flew to Sacramento, California, where the chimps lived. While Anne sat with Tracker, the owner of the chimps carried the youngest one, a two-year-old, into the room. He sat holding the little chimp while Anne stayed with Tracker. The chimp and the dog looked at each other. Tracker's tail wagged. The chimp leaned toward him. Clearly, the animals were curious, and each wanted to go closer to the other.

The two owners cautiously allowed the animals to approach each other. Soon the baby chimp was hanging on Tracker's tail and then sitting on his back. Tracker appeared to enjoy the fun as much as the chimp did.

One by one, the older chimps were also introduced.

Tracker got along fine with all of them. He and Anne flew back home, where Anne spent the next six weeks preparing Tracker to do his role.

Because Tracker's role required a lot of running, Anne needed a second dog to act as his double. This was in case they had to shoot some of the running scenes over and over. She did not want Tracker to get too tired, and she had no way to control how many times the scenes would need to be repeated.

It was not easy to find another dog who looked even remotely like Tracker. With his thoroughly mixed heritage, he has a one-of-a-kind appearance, which is what attracted the movie's director in the first place.

After a lengthy search, Anne finally borrowed a dog named Scooter from a friend. Scooter had been adopted from the Oregon Humane Society in Portland where Anne's friend worked.

Scooter closely matched Tracker in size and shape, and the coloring on her face was similar. Best of all, she had received both obedience and agility training. With natural vegetable dyes, Scooter's fur was darkened in places to make her look more like Tracker.

Anne, the two dogs, and an assistant trainer drove from Seattle to Saskatoon, Saskatchewan, in Canada, where the movie was to be filmed. They settled into a lakeside cabin that had been rented for them. The next day they drove past wheat and canola fields to the studio.

Tracker met Corey Sevier, the boy who would play the lead role in *Summer of the Monkeys*. Corey also had acted in the television series *Lassie*, so he was experienced at working with a dog.

Six chimps were on location to play the four chimps in the film. Just as Tracker needed a double to be sure he did not get overtired, the chimps had extra help, too. Anne and the owner of the chimps did not want to harm their animal friends. The American Humane Association also watches out for the welfare of all animal actors while they are at work on a movie or TV set.

For an animal, the hardest part of acting is to concentrate only on the trainer. This is especially difficult when more than one animal is in a project.

Tracker had several scenes with the chimps. He had to watch Anne and obey her signals without getting distracted by the chimps. They were nearby with *their* trainer, who was also giving them hand signals.

After six weeks of rehearsal, the filming began. All went smoothly until the scene which required a chimp to run out of the woods toward the camera. A few seconds later, Tracker was to chase the chimp. The chimp was supposed to look scared of the dog and run away as fast as he could.

The cameras rolled. The chimp was released. The chimp's trainer stood behind the camera, giving the hand signal to the chimp for him to come. The chimp obeyed and ran toward the camera—until Tracker was released behind him.

As soon as the chimp heard Tracker running after him, he stopped and waited for his friend. Dog and chimp then tore around in circles, playing happily with each other!

It took several retakes before the scene captured on film looked as if the chimp, terrified, was running from the dog.

Twice, the filming of scenes where Tracker had to run for a long distance had to be repeated so many times that Anne called for Scooter to take Tracker's place while Tracker rested.

When the filming ended, Scooter went home to Portland, and Tracker and Anne returned to their woodland home. Tracker seemed glad to see all the other animals again. He got a well-earned rest while he waited for the next call for an animal actor with his special looks and skills.

Tracker began life unwanted and unloved, as do far too many puppies. Every animal shelter staff member has heard the words, "I can't find homes for them all" hundreds of times.

Luckily for Tracker, he was taken to the Humane Society, where volunteer foster parents open their homes and hearts to puppies who are too young to be adopted. Because Tracker's foster parents held him, petted him, and kept him warm and fed, he developed into a happy, sociable puppy who liked people and was trainable.

Now Tracker is a movie star with a loving trainer, unusual animal friends, and a long career ahead of him.

About the American Humane Association

Whenever an animal is used in a movie or on television, the American Humane Association (AHA) has a trained person on the set to oversee the animal's safety and well-being. The purpose is to be sure that no animal is killed or harmed for the sake of entertainment.

The Screen Actors' Guild and the Alliance of Motion Picture and Television Producers have an agreement that, when animals are used in a film, the AHA must be sent a script before filming starts. The AHA then helps figure out ways to shoot the scenes while protecting both the animals and the actors.

The filmmakers are provided with a list of tips on how to protect animals. Producers who follow the AHA's strict guidelines have the right to run a notice at the end of the film stating that no animals were harmed during production.

Sometimes there are scenes that look as if an animal is being hurt, but in reality the animal is computer-generated.

The American Humane Association was established in 1877. It began working to protect animals in films and TV shows in 1940, after a horse was deliberately killed during the filming of a movie. The AHA now has twenty-five trained staff members who monitor the use of animals in movie, television, and commercial productions.

Each year, the first week of May is "Be Kind to Animals Week," an event started by AHA in 1916. As part of this effort, AHA sponsors the Be Kind to Animals Kid Award, recognizing children who have demonstrated outstanding acts of kindness toward animals. For more information, contact:

The American Humane Association
63 Inverness Drive East
Englewood CO
80112-5117

You can visit AHA on the Internet at:
www. amerhumane.org

Kirby

ONE WORD SAVED A LIFE

Kirby enjoys his favorite activity: going for a walk with his owners, Nita Baker and Helen Hughes, and their other dog, Sonny. Humane Society vet Dr. Bill Larson comes along.

3

~

FOR A LONG TIME, Kirby lived happily with his elderly owner. Then Kirby's owner became very sick. By the time he got to the hospital, he was too ill to tell anyone that his little dog was home alone.

Kirby, a small tan-colored terrier mix, wandered through his home, looking for his owner. He could not get outside to relieve himself, yet he had been taught not to go in the house. Why didn't his owner come to take him for a walk? He became more and more uncomfortable and nervous. Finally, he couldn't wait any longer. He had to relieve himself indoors.

A day and a night went by. No one came to feed him and his stomach hurt from hunger. Where was his dinner? Where was his owner? Kirby licked the last of the water from his bowl.

Another day and another night passed. Still no one came. Now Kirby paced anxiously, becoming more and more fearful.

In the hospital, Kirby's owner grew even sicker.

Kirby waited, alone and afraid.

His owner died.

After six long days, two social workers went to the home and found the little dog. A neighbor told them his name.

By then Kirby had suffered so much physical discomfort and emotional stress that he didn't trust anyone. He snarled and snapped. The social workers threw a blanket on him and tried to pick him up. He bit them both.

Eventually they managed to get him into a small carrier and took him to the Humane Society. The social workers, still bleeding, were glad to get rid of him.

All dogs who arrive at the Humane Society are checked by the veterinary staff, but Kirby was too upset to be handled. He growled and refused to come out of the carrier. The staff tried hard to calm Kirby and coax him out, but they failed.

Dr. Bill Larson, the veterinarian on duty, estimated that Kirby was about five years old.

Still in the carrier, Kirby was taken to the quiet hospital kennels, where animals are kept until they are well enough to be put up for adoption. Most of the animals in the hospital ward have a physical illness. Kirby's problem was emotional.

Kirby's carrier was put in a private kennel, and the door to the carrier was left open. Dr. Larson and the rest of the Humane Society staff hoped that plenty of food, water, and love would help Kirby heal from his terrible ordeal.

But Kirby seemed unable to forget his terror; he refused all efforts to comfort him. He stayed in the small carrier, growling and snapping when anyone approached. Each time fresh food was brought, Kirby cowered and bared his fangs. People had let Kirby down, and he apparently wanted nothing more to do with any human.

When Kirby arrived, Nita Baker was the senior veterinary technician at the Humane Society. After ten years there, she had a talent for calming the most ferocious dogs, and she had often succeeded with dogs who had not responded well to other people.

She decided to give Kirby some special attention.

Several times each day, Nita approached Kirby's kennel. When she tried to let Kirby sniff her hand, he retreated, huddling in the corner of the carrier and growling. She took him tasty dog treats; Kirby growled at her. She spoke softly and told him what a wonderful dog he was; Kirby snapped at her. When she tried to pet him, Kirby bared his teeth and Nita had to back away. No matter how hard Nita tried, nothing worked.

Clearly, Kirby was miserable. He was a beautiful little dog who looked as if he had once been loved and cared for; everyone hoped that they could somehow break through his distrust.

Nita kept trying for four days, and so did the rest of the staff, including Dr. Larson and Nita's friend, Helen Hughes, who worked in the adoption center. Kirby stayed fearful and unapproachable.

The saddest decision that the Humane Society staff must make is the decision to end an animal's life. But they know that a dog who snaps and snarls at everyone who comes near him cannot be put up for adoption. And it was obvious that the unhappy little terrier no longer enjoyed his life.

The staff decided that Kirby was not going to

recover from his terrible ordeal, and that euthanasia would be the kindest option. Much as they wanted a different outcome, they all agreed that this was best for Kirby.

Nita was assigned to assist Dr. Larson with the euthanasia. Because they wished they didn't have to do it, they put off going to Kirby's kennel until the very end of the day.

With heavy hearts, Nita and Dr. Larson put on thick leather gloves to protect themselves from Kirby's teeth. They took tools to dismantle the carrier that Kirby refused to leave and towels to put over him to help subdue him long enough to put a leash on him.

When they got to Kirby's kennel, he reacted as usual: he barked fiercely, snarled, and backed away.

Nita's eyes filled with tears as she looked at the sad little dog. She had tried so hard to save him, and she had failed.

Nita and Dr. Larson slipped inside the kennel and, using a screwdriver, took all the nuts and bolts off the carrier. They planned to use the carrier door as a shield in case Kirby attacked.

With the carrier dismantled, Nita managed to loop a leash around Kirby's neck. When Kirby felt the leash, he stopped struggling and stood still, looking perplexed.

Nita squatted down to be at his level, but she stayed the leash length away in case he tried to bite her. Kirby stood quietly and stared at her. Dr. Larson watched nervously, warning Nita to be careful.

Nita said softly, "Hey, Kirby. Want to go for a walk?"

When Kirby heard the word *walk*, he wagged his tail. He cocked his head, looking excited and enthusiastic. There was no snarling, no snapping, and no backing away.

Nita and Dr. Larson stared in disbelief.

Nita repeated the question. "Walk? Shall we go for a walk?"

Kirby's eyes lit up, and he quivered in anticipation.

Nita stood up and led Kirby out of the kennel and into the outdoor exercise yard. Kirby trotted along beside her. After a few laps around the yard, Nita removed the leash and tossed a tennis ball. Kirby ran after it and brought it back. When he dropped the ball at Nita's feet, she reached out to pat him, and Kirby wriggled with pleasure.

They continued the game of catch until Kirby grew tired. Then Nita sat on the walkway, and Kirby climbed into her lap for a snuggle. Nita stroked his fur, scratched behind his ears, and rubbed his tummy. Kirby licked her under her chin, his tail wagging.

Once again Nita's eyes filled with tears, but this time they were tears of joy. When she looked at Dr. Larson, he was crying, too. The little dog, who just hours before had seemed totally unadoptable, was suddenly a loving companion. All it took was a word he recognized.

Dr. Larson canceled the euthanasia order. The entire staff rejoiced.

Kirby still had a major problem, however. Because he had recently bitten the two social workers, he could not be put out for adoption.

Nita and Helen are foster parents for the Humane Society. They often take home dogs who need special care until they are ready to go into a permanent adoptive home. Nita and Helen decided to take Kirby home for a few days. They thought if they "fostered" Kirby for a while, it would help him regain his emotional health. If they could establish that Kirby was now unlikely to bite anyone, he might still be adoptable.

When Nita and Helen brought Kirby home, their own dog, who weighed one hundred pounds, and their three cats paid little attention to the newcomer. They were used to foster animals coming and going.

Kirby wasn't scared of the big dog and he didn't mind the cats. Whenever visitors came, Kirby barked, then wagged his tail when they greeted him. There was no growling and no snapping.

Nita doesn't know what prompted her that night to ask the little dog if he wanted to go for a walk. Habit? Intuition? Plain good luck? Whatever it was, she is thankful she said the magic word that released Kirby from his fear.

A few days became a few weeks, and then a few months. By then, Nita and Helen loved Kirby far too much to ever give him up. They adopted him permanently. And no matter how busy Nita and Helen are, they take Kirby for a walk, every single day.

Reminders from the Humane Society

1. If all dogs were allowed to breed unrestricted, there would be fifteen dogs born for every human in America. As it is, more than seven million unwanted pets are euthanized in America each year. The surgery to spay or neuter your dog so he or she can't produce puppies is a simple procedure. Spayed or neutered dogs are less likely to roam, and their chances of developing certain cancers and other diseases are reduced.

2. Your dog needs access at all times to fresh water and shade.

3. Loose dogs are often injured or stolen. They sometimes eat poisonous material such as antifreeze, or they get attacked by larger animals. Keep your dog safe by keeping him on a leash or in a fenced enclosure at all times.

4. Never leave a dog in a parked car, even with the windows open a crack. On a hot day, the temperature inside the car can quickly reach 120 degrees and cause heatstroke, brain damage, and death.

5. It is unsafe (and in many states illegal) to let a dog ride loose in the back of a pickup truck. Confine the dog to a crate that is secured to the truck bed or side.
6. Always keep a seven-day supply of dry dog food and bottled water on hand. In case of emergency or natural disaster, your dog will have enough to eat and drink.

Joey

INTERNATIONAL SERVICE DOG

Susan Duncan's service dog, Joey, pulls out a dishrack from the dishwasher at Susan's home. It is one of the many ordinary chores Joey does to help Susan, who has multiple sclerosis.

4

JOEY IS PART GERMAN SHEPHERD and part unknown. Both parts are huge. The woman who brought him to the Humane Society had found him running loose on a busy street so she knew nothing about his background. She kept him while she ran a "Found" ad in the paper and put up posters, but nobody claimed Joey.

There was no evidence that he had ever been housebroken or given any kind of training, and he had not been neutered.

Joey's teeth provided the best clue to his age: they showed he was about three years old. Only one thing about him was known for sure—he had plenty of energy. He jumped, tugged on the leash, and tried to investigate everything in the room while the woman who had found him signed the surrender papers.

A large, exuberant, untrained dog is not the first choice for most people who come looking for a companion animal. Joey's chances for adoption seemed slight.

Joey received the same care that all incoming dogs get. He was checked by a veterinarian, vaccinated, and sprayed for fleas. He was given a clean kennel and nourishing food while he waited for a new family. Occasionally, he was taken outside to the penned "Get Acquainted" area, where he raced wildly around.

Joey had been at the Humane Society for thirty-eight days when Susan Duncan came to the shelter. Susan has multiple sclerosis, a nerve disease that causes increasing weakness. She has lost much of the use of her left side. Her beloved nine-year-old service dog, Casper, had died unexpectedly two days earlier.

A service dog is any dog trained to perform tasks for a person with a disability. Some are guide dogs who help people with impaired vision; some are "hearing-ear" dogs who aid people with impaired hearing. Some do a variety of jobs for owners such as Susan.

Susan knew that most service dogs are purebreds, trained by professional service-dog trainers. However, there was a waiting period of at least a year to receive such a dog. Susan didn't want to give up a year or more of independence.

She had found Casper at the Humane Society. He was the family pet until Susan fell one day and was unable to get up. Casper went to her, rolled her onto her right side, and then tugged on her sleeve, pulling her to a sitting position so she could lean on him while she got to her feet. He had never been taught to do this.

Susan falls often. Until that day, she had always had to wait until another person could help her get back up. From then on, she depended on Casper to help her. She decided to try to train him to assist her in other ways.

She called a professional service-dog trainer for advice and was told she would not be able to train a dog herself. Undaunted, Susan read animal training books and began working with Casper, using simple commands and praising him when he did what she wanted. She taught him to hold doors open for her and pick up items she dropped. He learned to let her lean on him for balance as she got in and out of bed. He became her constant companion.

Now Casper was gone, and Susan was trying to put

aside her grief. She knew she needed a new dog, so once again she went to the Humane Society.

She paused in front of Joey's kennel and gazed at the large brown-and-black dog. One of his ears stuck out sideways and the other flopped forward. He seemed eager and alert, and he was tall enough that she could rest a hand on his shoulder when he stood beside her. Susan decided to take Joey into the Get Acquainted area.

When she opened the kennel door to put a leash on him, Joey leaped up and placed his front paws on Susan's shoulders. Susan staggered backwards, dropped her cane, and stepped in Joey's water bowl.

Joey wagged his tail. Susan realized that, on two legs, he was taller than she was, and he weighed more than she did. She wondered if this was such a good idea after all. She managed to get the leash on Joey and somehow kept her balance as he tugged her toward the door.

In the Get Acquainted area, Joey chased a tennis ball while Susan debated. Could she successfully train such a big, energetic dog? Although she liked his playful personality, she decided to think it over.

The next day Susan brought her husband and two

daughters to meet Joey. As usual, he galloped wildly around the Get Acquainted pen, but he was careful not to bump into anyone, and he was gentle with the children.

The family vote was unanimous: yes. Joey was neutered that same afternoon and went home with Susan the next day.

His training started immediately. Susan began with the basics, teaching Joey not to jump on people, to come when called, to lie down and stay, and to heel. He seemed eager to please and learned quickly.

Joey accepted wearing his service-dog pack right away. The pack is a sturdy red-and-black bag that fits over his back like a saddle. In it, Joey carries Susan's wallet, his official service-dog identification, and anything else Susan needs to take with her. He also carries items she purchases.

From the start, Joey went to Susan immediately when she fell and let her lean on him while she pulled herself upright. Now he also puts his snout under her chin and pushes her head up. If necessary, he rolls her from her weak left side to her stronger right side.

Other tasks took longer to master. For each job, Susan gave a command and tried to show him what she wanted. When Joey did it right, she praised him. If he did something else, she repeated the command and showed him again until Joey caught on. Every time he obeyed she told him what a good dog he was. She practiced each job with him many times before going on to teach him a new skill.

Now he tugs on her sleeves and pant legs to help her get her clothing on or off. He knows how to pull her socks off her feet and toss them into her lap. When the telephone rings, Joey lifts the receiver in his mouth and holds it until Susan can get there. He pulls cords to open cupboards, drawers, and the dishwasher.

As a service dog, Joey is permitted in public places such as grocery stores, restaurants, movie theaters, and hotels. He has learned to ride an escalator and not to lick babies and small children, no matter how good they smell!

Joey goes grocery shopping with Susan. If she needs an item from a shelf that's too low for her to reach, she points to it and Joey gets it for her. He sometimes carries groceries to the checkout stand in his pack, and he brings them into the house when he and Susan get home.

She often leans on him to keep her balance. He

holds doors open. When she drops her cane, Joey picks it up. If he were not there, she would need to ask for help.

Without Joey, Susan could not even go to the bathroom alone. He stands beside her so that she can keep her balance when she sits down. She grasps him to pull herself back to a standing position.

Susan is able to go swimming at a club because Joey is there to help her get in and out of the pool. With Joey at her side, she volunteers at her daughters' schools.

People who are familiar with guide dogs for the blind or hearing-ear dogs for the deaf are often startled to realize that Susan can see and hear just fine. Since most service dogs are purebred German shepherds, golden retrievers, or Labrador retrievers, Joey's obvious mixed heritage also creates interest. Susan is frequently stopped by strangers and asked to explain Joey's background and purpose.

Susan works from her home office as a nurse educator, planning courses for medical students. Because of Joey, she is able to attend meetings and give lectures that are important to her career.

One day Susan was contacted by Chris Lehman, a woman who also has multiple sclerosis. Chris had a service dog trained by an organization, and she was curious to know how Susan had trained Joey herself. The two women met and talked while their dogs played together.

Chris told Susan about the Delta Society, a non-profit organization that promotes the human health benefits of animals. The Delta Society sponsors a national Service Dog of the Year Award. Chris nominated Joey for the award. When the Humane Society staff saw what an excellent service dog Joey had become, they also nominated him.

Hundreds of fine service dogs from all over the country were nominated for this special honor.

Joey won!

The award was presented in New York City. Joey flew from Seattle to New York with Susan, sitting in the cabin of the airplane with her as is permitted by law for service dogs. He stayed with her at a fancy hotel where he shook hands with the doorman and charmed the staff.

While in New York, Joey and Susan were interviewed by newspaper and television reporters, and Joey demonstrated some of his skills on national TV. CNN did a story about Joey and Susan which was picked up by several airlines for use as an informational public service feature.

The news spread. An ordinary mutt from a shelter had been trained by a person with disabilities to do complicated tasks so well that he had won the Service Dog of the Year award. Thousands of people learned that an older, mixed-breed dog was capable of learning difficult jobs.

Susan began volunteering with the Delta Society, answering calls about service dogs. Most calls were from disabled people who wanted information about these valuable animals, but many calls also came from business people who needed to know how to treat their customers who used a service dog.

People with service dogs are often refused admittance to businesses because the people who work there do not know that service dogs are allowed, by law, to accompany their owners in public places.

Susan is now coordinator of the Delta Society's National Service Dog Center. This organization tells people how they can get a service dog, refers them to trainers, and teaches businesses how to accommodate people with service dogs. Its goal is to make more service dogs available and to educate the public so that service dogs are accepted. The Service Dog Center presently receives more than fourteen thousand inquiries each year.

Susan also writes model service-dog policies for businesses and other organizations, such as the Washington State Department of Transportation.

Before she became ill with multiple sclerosis, Susan worked as a registered nurse. Back then, even though she met many disabled people, she did not know about service dogs. Now she hopes to help educate as many people as possible.

A year after Joey won his award, Susan was asked to give a presentation at the Delta Society's international convention in Geneva, Switzerland. Once again, Joey boarded an airplane with his mistress, this time to fly across the Atlantic.

As Susan stood outside a meeting room at the convention, she was approached by a Japanese woman who asked, "Are you Susan Duncan?"

When Susan said yes, the woman introduced herself as Dr. Takayanagi, a physician. "I saw you on television during my flight here from Japan," she said.

Dr. Takayanagi had seen the CNN clip from Joey's New York visit, and she was excited to meet Susan in person. She told Susan that in Japan service dogs are too expensive for the average person. She hoped to change that, and she thought Susan could help.

The doctor invited Susan and Joey to go to Japan so that Susan could give a series of talks about how she had trained Joey herself.

Joey became the first service dog to travel to Japan. He wore a pack with "Service Dog" written on it in Japanese. He and Susan stayed two weeks and were the subject of a television documentary about how service dogs can help disabled people.

Joey has also been to Spain, where he and Susan stayed in a small village right on the shore of the Mediterranean Sea. Medical professionals from throughout Spain gathered there to hear Susan speak. When she and Joey demonstrated all the things he does to assist her, even those in the audience who could not understand English knew exactly what Susan meant.

Not all of Joey's trips have been for business. He has also vacationed in Disney World with Susan and her family. There he had his picture taken wearing mouse ears!

When Joey is at home, he often naps on his special pad on the living room floor. Like most well-loved family dogs, he enjoys frequent hugs and has many toys. He barks if a visitor rings the doorbell and stands protectively beside Susan when she opens the door. He sleeps next to her bed.

When Susan went to the Humane Society looking for a potential service dog, Joey was untrained, unruly, and large. Thanks to Susan's determination and to Joey's intelligence and aptitude for service work, he is now a world traveler with an important job.

About Service Dogs

If you see someone with a service dog, be sure to ask permission before you pet or talk to the dog. The dog is working, and it may be important not to distract him.

To learn more about service dogs, contact:
    National Service Dog Center
    289 Perimeter Road East
    Renton WA 98055-1329

The Delta Society can be reached at the above address or at:
    300 Park Avenue, 2nd Floor
    New York NY 10022-7499

You can also visit the Delta Society at:
    www.deltasociety.org

Danny

OVERCOMING FEARS

Jessica Mitchell leads Danny through the "Dawg Gone Days" 4-H qualifying obedience competition in Enumclaw, Washington. They are trying for a spot at the Washington State Fair in Puyallup.

5

WHEN JESSICA MITCHELL was three years old, she went to visit her grandmother. Her uncle was also visiting that day. He had brought along his dog, a pit bull.

Pit bull terriers, commonly known as pit bulls, were originally bred to fight. Although pit bulls can be gentle, many are used as guard dogs and are sometimes trained to be aggressive.

As little Jessica ran up the sidewalk toward her grandmother's house, her uncle's dog attacked her. Jessica screamed with pain and fear as the dog knocked her down and bit her many times in the face and around her eyes.

Police and paramedics raced to the scene. Sirens wailing, an ambulance rushed Jessica to the hospital.

She went immediately into surgery, where doctors rebuilt her torn cheek and put her jaw muscle back together. Jessica spent a week in the hospital. Her wounds were painful, but eventually they healed, leaving a lot of scar tissue.

When Jessica was in first grade, she was hospitalized again while doctors did reconstructive surgery to minimize a C-shaped scar around one eye. Later, another surgery removed excess scar tissue from her jaw. While her face looks fine, she may still need further surgery.

After she was attacked, Jessica became fearful of dogs. She liked other animals, and she understood that most dogs never attack anyone unless they are threatened themselves. Still, whenever she saw a dog, she felt panicky.

By the time Jessica was eight, she wanted to conquer her fear. Many of her friends had dogs, and Jessica longed to pet them and play with them without being frightened.

She didn't think she would feel threatened by a little puppy, so she asked her parents if she could have one. Mr. and Mrs. Mitchell agreed, and they took Jessica to the Humane Society.

One of the available puppies that day was a shepherd/Lab mix who was eight weeks old. Because he was brought to the shelter when he was too young to be adopted, he had been placed in a foster home, where he had received plenty of love and attention.

The pup was gentle and friendly and liked being held. The Humane Society staff thought he would be a good choice for Jessica, and Jessica thought so, too. She named him Danny and took him home.

Danny turned out to be the perfect puppy. His silliness made Jessica laugh. She liked to pet him and play with him. Danny gave her puppy kisses and napped on her lap.

Of course he grew bigger, but Jessica already loved and trusted him. She had nothing to fear, even when he was fully grown. Although the rest of Jessica's family enjoyed Danny, too, he seemed to know that he was Jessica's dog.

While she felt completely comfortable with Danny, Jessica still had twinges of fear when she met other dogs.

A year after she adopted Danny, Jessica joined 4-H, an international program for young people. The 4-H club emblem is a four-leaf clover. The four Hs stand for head, heart, hands, and health.

All 4-H members select a project to work on. Jessica could choose from dozens of possible subjects, including plant science, computers, performing arts, geology, and woodworking. Because Jessica was having so much fun with Danny, she chose "Companion Animals."

At weekly meetings, Jessica learned about vaccinations Danny needed, how to groom him, and how to control parasites such as fleas, ticks, and lice. She and Danny practiced basic obedience. He learned how to heel on a leash, how to stay, and how to follow other commands.

As they worked together, Jessica and Danny became even closer; each one trusted the other completely.

Of course, the other members of Jessica's 4-H dog group brought their dogs to the weekly meetings. Jessica got to know those dogs well and grew to like and trust them. Before long, she was no longer afraid of dogs.

Jessica also took a 4-H veterinary science class. She learned more about the health of her dog and became aware of career opportunities for working with animals.

Jessica's family had a fenced backyard with a locked gate so that Danny could spend time outdoors. One afternoon, the Mitchells left Danny in the backyard while they were away for a while.

Before, whenever they returned home, Danny had always run to greet them, happily wagging his tail. That day, when the family got home, Danny tried to hide behind a bush. Instead of flapping his tail from side to side as he usually did, he kept it tucked between his legs. He shook with fear.

The Mitchells took Danny inside and examined him carefully, but they couldn't find anything wrong. Jessica knew something had happened, but she had no way to find out what. Danny did not seem sick; he seemed terrified.

From then on, whenever anyone outside the family came to the door, Danny hid under the dining-room table, peeking nervously out at the visitor.

Jessica's formerly happy dog was now a fearful dog, and she had no idea why. Jessica gave him extra love and attention, as did her parents, but Danny continued to act frightened of strangers.

About this time one of the local utility companies was doing work in the Mitchells' neighborhood. A few days after Danny began acting scared, a worker from the utility company needed to go into the Mitchells' yard.

Danny was outside. Though he had been cowering at strangers, he barked ferociously at this man.

Jessica's father went to get Danny, to put him inside.

The worker said, "It's okay. If he gets near me, I'll just Mace him."

Mr. Mitchell knew that Mace, a chemical spray, is sometimes used to control mobs of people who are rioting. When Mace is sprayed in a person's face, it causes tears, dizziness, and nausea. The victim is usually temporarily unable to move.

Horrified, the Mitchells speculated about what might have happened on the day they were gone. Utility workers had been working in the neighborhood then, too. Had one of them climbed the fence to do work in the yard and then, when Danny approached, sprayed the dog with Mace? If so, it was no wonder Danny acted traumatized. And no wonder he was now afraid of everyone except his family.

Danny continued to act scared of everyone who came into Jessica's house. But when she took him to the 4-H meetings, he was excited and seemed happy to go. He acted glad to see the other dogs, and he clearly enjoyed the 4-H training.

Just as 4-H had been a way for Jessica to forget her fear of dogs she didn't know, 4-H became a way for Danny to get over his fear of people he didn't know.

In between 4-H meetings, Jessica and Danny

practiced all the obedience commands over and over. When Danny obeyed correctly, Jessica praised him or rewarded him with a small treat. Their practice sessions became a way to play together. Jessica kept records of his progress.

Danny did so well that Jessica decided it would be fun to show him in a 4-H dog show. Unlike most dog shows, 4-H shows do not require that the dogs be purebreds. In 4-H, the judging is based on the ability of the person showing the dog to control the dog and on the condition and grooming of the dog. A mixed breed like Danny has just as much chance of winning as a purebred does.

Jessica established a goal for herself and Danny: to compete in the 4-H dog show at the county fair. Before a 4-H member can show a dog at the fair, he or she must successfully complete two 4-H Fun Matches.

The Fun Matches are run like dog shows but are done just for practice, to get the dogs and their handlers accustomed to performing.

Jessica and Danny entered a 4-H Fun Match. The event was well-named; Jessica and Danny both had a great time. Danny loved being brushed and fussed over while Jessica waited for her turn to perform. Jessica liked watching the other 4-H kids and their dogs. Most of all, she enjoyed showing the judges how well Danny obeyed.

Danny heeled beautifully as he walked in with Jessica, sat down promptly on command, and stood motionless while the judge examined his fur.

The hardest part of the show for Danny was when the dogs were told to stay while the owners walked away from them. There were four dogs in Danny's group, and they were supposed to sit where they were until the judge told the owners to call them.

Jessica knew Danny wanted to be close to her when there were strangers present. After she gave him the stay command, she crossed her fingers while she went to the far side of the arena. Danny sat still, with his eyes focused on Jessica. Even when one of the other dogs got up before he was supposed to and ran to his owner, Danny remained where he was. When Jessica finally told him to come, Danny galloped happily to her side.

"Good dog," she told him. "Good, good dog!"

To Jessica's delight, she and Danny won second place. She received a rainbow-colored ribbon with a rosette.

Jessica entered another Fun Match, and this time

she received a first-place blue ribbon. She and Danny continued to practice. She groomed him daily.

They moved up to the novice class and then to graduate novice, where Danny had to know more difficult commands and be able to do them without a leash. They entered another match and another. They won more ribbons. Jessica and Danny made it to the county fair where they did so well that they qualified to go on to the state fair. There, the top two handlers each won a medallion with dogs on it. Jessica beamed with pride as the judge hung the beautiful medallion on its red-white-and-blue ribbon around her neck.

The crowd watching would never have imagined that this confident girl, who showed Danny with such poise, had once been terrified of dogs.

A vendor at the fair sold necklaces. One was a silver chain with a four-leaf clover on it. Purchasers could have their names engraved on the clover. Jessica bought a necklace, and she had two names engraved on it: Jessica and Danny.

He had rescued her from her fear of dogs, and she had rescued him from his fear of people. No wonder they are best friends now.

About 4-H Clubs

There are 4-H clubs in all fifty states and in eighty-two other countries. The members are divided by age level, with groups for students from kindergarten through twelfth grade.

To find a 4-H near you, contact:
National 4-H Council
7100 Connecticut Avenue
Chevy Chase MD 20815

About Preventing Dog Bites

1. Never go into a yard or reach through a car window to pet a dog you don't know. If the owner is there, ask permission to pet the dog.
2. Always be gentle and kind when you play with a dog.
3. Never grab anything such as a toy, ball, or bone from a dog.

4. If a dog growls or snarls at you with his teeth bared, he is getting ready to bite. It is also a warning if his legs are stiff and his ears are laid back.
5. If you think a dog might bite you, walk slowly away from him sideways. Do not turn your back and run away. Tell the dog "No!" but don't stare into his eyes.
6. If an angry dog ever jumps on you, curl into a ball and protect your face.

Tyler

THE DOG WHO COULDN'T SEE

At the home of Ann Graves and Donna Amos,
in Renton, Washington, Tyler makes sure that
a kitten from a foster litter gets clean.

6

TYLER IS A BORDER COLLIE, black with a white chest, white on his muzzle, and tips of white on his tail and feet. He was three years old when he and his sister, Tipper, were brought to the Humane Society.

Tyler and Tipper had always been barn dogs. They had never lived indoors, had not been house-trained, and except for being fed had received little human attention. Both dogs were matted and filthy.

Tyler was blind.

The owner's reason for giving them up was "They harass the chickens." When questioned, he stated that neither dog had ever killed a chicken or even caught one. What they actually did was try to herd the chickens.

"The one dog can't see," the owner added, as an afterthought. He had never taken Tyler to a veterinarian to have his eyes checked. "What for?" he asked. "He's blind."

Border collies are bred to work as herders, so it

was not surprising that Tyler and his sister had tried to herd the chickens. That fact did not make the dogs unacceptable as family pets. But Tyler's blindness would probably make it hard to find a home for him. With so many homeless dogs to choose from, few people will select one who can't see.

The day Tyler and Tipper came to the Humane Society, Ann Graves was helping in the veterinary department. Ann had recently left a successful career with United Parcel Service. Now she was in college, studying to become a veterinarian. Every Thursday, she volunteered at the Humane Society.

As Ann assisted Dr. Quinn, the vet who checked the two border collies, she was impressed by their sweet, gentle nature.

Special attention was paid to Tyler's white, cloudy-looking eyes.

"He can't see because he has cataracts," Dr. Quinn said. "If that's the only problem with his eyes, surgery might help. He needs to be seen by a vet who specializes in eye care."

Ann hoped that Tyler would find a home with someone who would take him to a veterinary eye specialist.

The two dogs were kenneled together. Tyler seemed to depend on Tipper to guide him, and everyone at the Humane Society hoped that someone would adopt both dogs.

The next week was that year's Tuxes and Tails fundraiser, and Ann was in charge of selecting which shelter dogs would appear at the annual event. Every year, professional groomers volunteer their services so that each dog will look his or her best. The dogs receive extra practice walking on a leash to get them ready for their big evening.

Three days before the auction, two of the dogs who had been prepared got adopted. Ann wondered about using Tipper and Tyler as their replacements. She knew that a fully grown blind dog who had never been house-trained was unlikely to get adopted. She decided the auction was Tyler's best chance. The audience would see his beauty and his loving personality; they would see how well he got along, with Tipper's help. Maybe someone would want both dogs.

Ann worried about how a blind dog would react to being in a crowd, especially a dog who was not used to people. She discussed her concerns with Dr. Quinn and the rest of the Humane Society staff. They agreed that the auction was the best opportunity for Tyler and Tipper to find a permanent home.

Ann took them to the groomer. When she went back to get them, the groomer said, "Those were the dirtiest dogs I've ever bathed."

Ann practiced leading the two dogs on leashes and discovered that as long as they were together, they did fine. When she tried to walk them separately, Tyler panicked and Tipper became extremely shy and nervous.

Ann gave special instructions to the volunteers who would be working with Tyler and Tipper at the auction: "The border collies *must* walk together down the runway."

Three celebrities from a local radio station were scheduled to go down the runway at the same time—two men who would have Tyler and Tipper on leashes, and a woman who would walk slightly behind the men and the dogs.

The volunteers got the dogs and celebrities in place. The announcer gave their names. And then, at the last second, there was a misunderstanding: the woman ended up with both dogs, while the men preceded her across the stage.

It is hard for one person to keep two excited dogs

under control. In the confusion, Tyler got too close to the edge of the stage. Unable to see, he toppled off.

Ann was backstage getting another dog ready to go on when her walkie-talkie blasted the news. "Ann! Tyler fell off the runway!"

Her heart in her throat, Ann rushed out in time to see a member of the audience lift Tyler back onto the stage. Tyler sniffed for Tipper, who was overjoyed to see him. Tyler wasn't hurt, and the two dogs finished walking down the runway and back with no more problems.

As the auction-goers filed out the door, they passed by all the dogs who had taken part in the event. Many people stopped to pet Tipper and Tyler and to talk with the volunteers about the two beautiful border collies. Ann pointed out that surgery might help Tyler's eyesight.

For the next few days, all the staff and volunteers waited, hoping that someone would want both dogs.

No one did.

Meanwhile, Ann and her partner, Donna Amos, talked about the possibility of taking Tipper and Tyler themselves. Donna had met them when she helped at Tuxes and Tails, and she agreed that they were special dogs. But Ann and Donna already had two dogs: Skip, a fourteen-year-old black Lab who had arthritis and back problems, and Blue, a nine-year-old Australian shepherd/Lab mix.

They worried that it might not be fair to elderly Skip to bring in another dog with medical problems. And they worried about their finances. As a college student, Ann's income was limited to part-time work. In addition to the dogs, Ann and Donna had two cats. They didn't see how they could afford to take care of another animal.

The week after the auction, Ann arrived at the Humane Society for her regular volunteer shift. She went out to the kennel to check on Tipper and Tyler—and found Tyler alone.

"Tipper got adopted yesterday," she was told. "She went to a good family, with children who are crazy about her."

"They didn't want both dogs?" Ann asked.

"They didn't want a blind dog."

Ann worried about Tyler all day. How could he possibly get along without his seeing-eye companion? It's hard enough for any animal to stay at the shelter. What must it be like for one who couldn't see? And now Tyler was left alone in this strange, noisy place, without the sister who had guided him for so long.

When Ann got home and told Donna what had happened, Donna said, "Go get him. We'll work it out somehow."

The next day, Ann brought Tyler home.

Ann and Donna are foster parents for the Humane Society, often raising litters of kittens who are too young when they're taken from their mothers. The two women also nurse injured dogs and cats back to health so that they can be adopted. Skip, Blue, and the two cats, Billy and Bear, were used to having animal visitors. They were not upset by the appearance of yet another dog.

Tyler cautiously sniffed his way around the house, staying in the center of each room so he wouldn't bump into any furniture. He passed the couch where Bear, Ann's eighteen-pound cat, was sleeping.

As he started past the cat, Tyler stopped and sniffed, putting his nose right on Bear. Then he stuck out his tongue and slurped Bear across the face.

Ann tensed, expecting Bear to hiss or scratch Tyler's nose. To her surprise, the cat seemed to realize that Tyler meant no harm. He just lay there while Tyler moved on. The same thing happened the first time

Tyler encountered Billy. Tyler sniffed and slurped; the cat tolerated it.

Skip often slept in the middle of the floor. More than once that first day, Tyler tripped on the inert Skip, startling both of them. Like the cats, Skip seemed to understand that Tyler didn't intend to annoy him. Skip never growled or snapped; he just stood up and moved aside so Tyler could go by.

Blue, on the other hand, wanted Tyler to play. He pranced in front of the newcomer with his upper body down and his tail wagging, inviting Tyler to chase him or to wrestle. Since Tyler could not see what Blue was doing, he made no response.

Finally Blue stopped and stared at Tyler, perplexed. In the next few days, Blue tried again and again to get Tyler to play. Tyler of course ignored him, and Blue finally gave up.

Tyler adjusted quickly to his new home. He had never encountered steps before, and there were four steps from the door to the yard. He hesitated the first few times but then seemed to remember exactly how many steps there were. From then on he went confidently up and down as if he were counting in his head.

When Tyler stumbled on a backpack that had been left on the floor, Ann and Donna quickly picked up all shoes, books, and any other objects that Tyler might trip over.

At first, Ann worried about a dog who had never been house-trained. She and Donna took Tyler outside as soon as he had eaten, and again every two or three hours. Although he had never lived indoors and had not been house-trained, he seemed to know what was expected. As long as he was put outside regularly, he never had an accident in the house.

Skip and Blue had a favorite outdoor game: Ann kicked a ball for them, and they chased it. While they played, Tyler stood patiently by Ann's side, waiting to go back indoors. He couldn't join in the game because he couldn't see the ball.

A few days after adopting Tyler, Ann took him to a veterinarian who specializes in eye problems. The diagnosis was cataracts, a clouding of the lens of the eye. Tyler may have had vision as a puppy, but now the vet said the dog was seeing the world as if he were looking through a windshield that had two feet of snow on it. Tests showed no other problem.

Cataracts, Ann learned, are common in border

collies. She also learned that surgery could correct the problem. Although it was expensive to have surgery on both eyes, Ann never hesitated.

"We'll do it," she told the vet, wondering how she and Donna would find the money to pay for it.

The cataract surgery was scheduled. In this operation, the cloudy lens is removed from each eye and replaced with a thin clear plastic lens. The same surgery is often performed on people.

On the morning of the surgery, Ann left Tyler at the veterinary clinic, hoping the operation would be successful.

When she went back a few hours later, Tyler was wearing a stiff plastic cone-shaped collar that surrounded his head like a large megaphone. The collar would prevent Tyler from scratching at his eyes or from bumping his head.

"Hello, Tyler," Ann said.

Tyler turned toward her voice, as he always did. And then he did something he had never done before: he walked straight toward her.

Tyler could see.

Ann knelt to look into his clear brown eyes. The white cloudiness was gone.

"The operation was a complete success," the vet said. "Tyler now has one hundred percent vision in both eyes."

Although Tyler was still groggy from the anesthetic, he began exploring the house as soon as Ann got him home. He went to Donna, sniffed her, and then looked hard as if putting together for the first time the familiar scent and the unfamiliar sight.

He walked all around the house, sniffing at objects and then pausing to look at them.

"We could almost see his brain computing as he put together the smells he recognized with the brand-new sights he was seeing," Ann recalls.

He walked past the couch where Bear, the cat, lay snoozing. Tyler stopped, smelled Bear, and stared at him with an expression of total astonishment on his face. Ann and Donna are sure he was thinking, "So that's what a cat looks like!"

Tyler had always walked with his tail tucked down between his legs, a sign of anxiety. It was as if he had tried to make himself as small as possible so that he wouldn't accidentally bump anything.

Now that he could see, he relaxed and began to hold his tail out in a normal position.

When Ann went to the Humane Society the next week, everyone rejoiced at the good news. Ann was handed an envelope full of money. Other volunteers had taken up a collection to help pay for Tyler's surgery.

The collar stayed on for several weeks while Tyler's eyes healed. During that time, Tyler continued to act amazed at the many things he could now see.

Before the surgery, when Tyler had heard a car outside, he would walk to the window, cock his head, and listen. The first time he heard a car after the surgery, he went to the window and then pressed his nose against the glass, staring as the car drove past. From then on, he spent many hours each day looking out the window.

About a month after the surgery, Ann had the three dogs in the yard. She kicked a ball and as always, Skip and Blue chased it. But this time, Tyler ran after them! His tail waved high in the air as he raced along with the other two dogs. For the first time since he had lost his sight, Tyler was playing.

He is now a regular part of the game. But unlike Skip and Blue, Tyler doesn't care about the ball. What he likes to do is herd the other dogs, trying to guide them toward the ball.

He tries to herd them in other situations, too. When

Ann comes home, Tyler runs behind Blue, making sure Blue goes straight to Ann.

Soon after Tyler's protective collar was removed, a new litter of kittens in need of foster care joined the household. Bottle-feeding a newborn kitten is a messy affair; usually the kitten's face is quickly covered with milk.

Tyler eagerly took over the job of cleaning up the kittens after they were fed. Just like a mother cat, he carefully licked the spilled milk from each tiny kitten's face. The kittens purred and snuggled close to him.

Tyler has continued to wash every litter of kittens that Ann and Donna have fostered. He also washes Skip's and Blue's ears each night before they go to bed.

Tyler endured three years of neglect. He was blind, afraid, and separated from his sister, the only companion he had ever known. Yet he remained trusting and gentle.

Ann says, "Tyler loves the baby kittens, the other dogs, the cats, us, and all our visitors. We're so happy that he can finally see the world he loves."

About a Dog's Eyesight

Dogs can see better in the dark than humans can, but they do not see colors as clearly as we do.

Dogs' eyes are sensitive to movement; when something moves, they see it more clearly than when it is still.

One way to test your dog's eyesight is to stand a few feet in front of her and drop a cotton ball. Do it several times. If your dog doesn't look at the cotton ball as it falls, she probably can't see it.

If you suspect that your dog has trouble seeing, take her to your veterinarian. Eye problems might be a symptom of a treatable disease.

Ivan

FIRE-ALARM HERO

Alexandra Brumleve hugs the family dog, American Red Cross Animal Hero Ivan, as Alexandra's mother, Taj Brumleve, looks on. Photograph by David Harrison.

7

*T*AJ BRUMLEVE IS LEGALLY DEAF. She cannot hear a telephone ringing or someone knocking at her door. She cannot hear the high-pitched sound of a smoke alarm going off. She cannot hear when her daughter, Alexandra, cries or calls to her.

When Alexandra was two, Taj decided to get a hearing-ear dog who would let her know when Alexandra needed her or when the phone or doorbell rang. Since there was a long waiting period to receive such a service dog, Taj decided to try to train a dog herself. She had always loved animals and knew she would like the companionship of a dog even if the home training didn't work out.

Although most hearing-ear dogs are purebreds, Taj decided to get her dog from an animal shelter. She wanted to adopt a dog who would otherwise not have a home.

Taj went to the King County Animal Shelter in Kent,

Washington. The shelter had a nine-week-old puppy, part black Labrador and part Siberian husky, who had been brought in because the owner couldn't find a home for him.

The puppy was coal black with expressive golden eyes and a friendly personality. Taj knew he would grow to be a large dog, and that was okay.

She named him Ivan and took him home. Alexandra loved the puppy, and Ivan quickly became a cherished member of the household. Even Taj's cat, Orca, enjoyed watching Ivan play.

Like any puppy, Ivan required a lot of attention and training. At first, Taj concentrated on house-training him. When that was accomplished, she began teaching him hand signals for "sit" and "come."

As Ivan grew, he seemed to sense that Taj could not hear. When he wanted her attention, he didn't bark; instead, he went to her and nudged her.

A year after they adopted Ivan, Taj and her husband rented a new townhome. Alexandra got her own bedroom, and there was more room for Ivan, who was now fully grown. By then the Brumleves had learned that Alexandra was hearing-impaired like her mother, so Ivan's training and duties became even more important. He now had two deaf people to watch out for.

One afternoon Taj put three-year-old Alexandra in her bed for a nap. Then Taj went downstairs, with Ivan at her side. She stretched out on the couch in the living room and fell asleep. Ivan, as always, lay on the floor next to her.

Taj was sleeping soundly when she felt something heavy on her chest. Still half-asleep, she realized it was Ivan. Ivan weighed sixty pounds, so she definitely did not want him sitting on her.

He licked her face and pawed at her arm.

"Ivan, get down," she said sleepily, pushing the dog to the floor. It took her a few minutes to wake up fully, but when she did, she realized that Ivan would never jump on her unless something was wrong.

She opened her eyes. Ivan was no longer beside her.

The room looked foggy, and she now smelled smoke. Fear jolted through Taj.

Fire!

She leaped off the couch.

Knowing Alexandra would not hear her call, Taj raced for the stairs. The thick smoke made her cough. Her eyes smarted, and her heart pounded with fear for her little girl.

When she reached the bottom of the stairs, she met Ivan—with Alexandra at his side! Ivan had Alexandra's shirt sleeve in his mouth. He was tugging the sleepy child forward toward the front door!

As soon as he knew Taj was awake, Ivan had gone upstairs to awaken Alexandra and lead her to safety.

Knowing that her daughter was safe, Taj quickly searched for the cause of the smoke, thinking she might be able to put the fire out. Nothing was burning in the kitchen. She hurried back to the stairway and looked up. Smoke billowed from around the sides of Alexandra's bedroom door.

Taj now knows that she should have taken Alexandra and Ivan outside immediately and stayed out herself. But that day she was only thinking of trying to put out the fire. She left Alexandra and Ivan downstairs and rushed up to Alexandra's room. She put her hands on the door and then jerked them back. The door was too hot to open.

She peered through the keyhole and saw nothing but blackness. Alexandra's bedroom was so full of smoke that Taj could not even see the outline of the bed.

"It was like looking into space," Taj says.

She raced back down the stairs. By then the house was so full of smoke she could barely breathe. Taj grabbed Alexandra's hand and scooped up the terrified Orca. With Ivan following, they ran to their neighbor's home.

"Fire!" Taj screamed as she pounded on the neighbor's door.

The neighbor called 911. She kept Alexandra, Ivan, and Orca inside. Taj called her husband, Michael, at work and he rushed home.

Taj couldn't hear the wail of the approaching sirens, but she saw the fire trucks roar up the street. She watched as the firefighters aimed their hoses at her home.

Horrified, she saw the firefighters pull a burning mattress out of the house. Alexandra had been napping on that mattress. Taj knew that sleeping people are sometimes overcome by smoke inhalation; they never wake up to flee from the fire.

Tears streamed down her face as she thought what would have happened to Alexandra if Ivan had not smelled the smoke and jumped on Taj to wake her up. What if he had not gone up the stairs and entered that smoke-filled bedroom? What if he had not taken the little girl's sleeve in his mouth and tugged until she followed him down the stairs?

"Another fifteen minutes," Taj says, "and Alexandra and I almost certainly would have been overcome by smoke. We probably wouldn't have made it."

Thanks to Ivan, the firefighters arrived in time to extinguish the blaze before it spread to the rest of the house. Taj and Alexandra had some breathing problems from inhaling smoke, but they recovered fully by the next day.

When the fire was finally out, Taj and Michael gathered basic necessities and prepared to move temporarily to the Westin Hotel in Seattle, where Michael worked. Taj made sure to take Ivan's blue food dish along.

The fire happened on the day before Thanksgiving; Ivan was fifteen months old.

On Thanksgiving Day, as Taj and Michael looked at what was left of their smoke-blackened home, they gave thanks that Ivan had saved Alexandra and Taj.

The Brumleves lost nearly seven thousand dollars worth of belongings, including Alexandra's bed and most of her toys and books. They had just finished painting and decorating the child's bedroom; now it was destroyed by smoke and water damage. But the losses seemed unimportant compared to the tragedy they might have faced.

Investigators said the fire started in Alexandra's room and speculated that she might have been playing with matches.

Because of her hearing impairment, Alexandra still had a limited vocabulary. She couldn't tell anyone exactly what had happened. Regardless of how the fire began, one fact was clear: Ivan first woke Taj, and then raced upstairs to get Alexandra.

"That dog saved the mother's life and the child's life," says Steve Gengo of the Redmond, Washington, Fire Department. "He acted on instinct; he saved his family."

Each year the Seattle/King County chapter of the American Red Cross has a "Heroes Breakfast" to pay tribute to ordinary people who have performed unusual acts of courage or kindness. A year after the fire, the Red Cross honored Ivan as an Animal Hero.

By then the Brumleves had moved to Kansas, but Taj brought Ivan back to Seattle to receive his award. Ivan sat in the seat next to hers for the plane ride and was given a set of wings by the captain.

At the award breakfast, Ivan wore a vest and bow tie. He seemed to enjoy all the attention and wagged his tail happily at the crowd.

Taj gave Ivan's acceptance speech for him. "The lesson that should come out of this," she said, "is that if you love your animals, they will love you."

Besides his Red Cross award, Ivan was honored by Heinz Pet Products, which gave him a six-month supply of dog food and a certificate of merit.

Ivan continues to be both a hearing-ear dog and a beloved pet for Taj and Alexandra. "To me," says Taj, "Ivan is the most wonderful mutt in the world."

About Fire Prevention

Fire destroys more property and claims more lives each year than tornadoes, floods, or any other natural disaster. Most fire fatalities and injuries in the United States occur in the victim's own home. Here are some things you can do to keep yourself and your family safe:

1. Make sure every level of your home has a working smoke detector.
2. Be sure your house numbers can be seen from the street.
3. Have a fire extinguisher in your kitchen.
4. Never leave cooking food unwatched.
5. If you see a fire in your home, get out immediately. It is too dangerous to telephone for help from a burning home. Call 911 on a neighbor's phone.
6. The American Society for the Prevention of Cruelty to Animals has stickers to put on or near entry doors to alert firefighters that animals are inside. The stickers provide space for you to write a phone number to be called in case of emergency. You can learn more about this organization at www.aspca.org or write to:

   ASPCA
   442 E. 92nd St.
   New York NY 10128

Bridgette

SEIZURE-ALERT DOG

Cliff Chartrand relaxes at his Richland, Washington,
home with Bridgette, his seizure-alert dog.

8

*T*HE BLACK-AND-WHITE DOG had no name. The person who owned her had never bothered to give her one.

When the dog had fourteen puppies, her owner found homes for six of them. The remaining eight, along with the mother dog, were taken to the Oregon Humane Society in Portland, Oregon.

With silky fur, large ears, and a flowing tail, the mother dog appeared to be mostly border collie, with some spaniel and sheltie mixed in. She had not been house-trained, nor had she ever received any other kind of training. She seemed to be about two years old.

A staff member named her Bridgette.

The puppies were weaned and put up for adoption. Bridgette was put up for adoption, too.

Andrea Wall is a volunteer at the Oregon Humane Society. She soon noticed Bridgette standing at the front of her kennel, with her big ears perked up. Bridgette watched everyone and listened to everything.

Andrea thought she seemed particularly intelligent.

Andrea had been on the lookout for exceptionally alert shelter dogs ever since she had met Jeanne Hampl. Jeanne had gone into a pet store one Saturday when Andrea had a shelter dog there as part of an Oregon Humane Society adoption program.

Jeanne introduced herself as the director of the Prison Pet Partnership Program (PPPP) at a women's prison. "We take dogs from animal rescue organizations," she said, "and give them the opportunity to lead lives of service. They are trained by the prison inmates to be service dogs for people with disabilities or therapy dogs for people who will benefit from the animal-human bond."

Intrigued, Andrea asked many questions. She learned that the Prison Pet Partnership Program was begun by Sister Pauline, a nun who believes that working with dogs helps people who must live in an institution, including those who are serving prison sentences.

In 1981, Sister Pauline got permission and funding to try her ideas at the Washington State Correctional Center for Women in Gig Harbor, Washington. The program proved so successful that it quickly expanded.

The prison now operates a full-service boarding kennel and offers grooming for all breeds. The inmate employees are certified as pet care technicians and/or groomers. Money earned from the boarding and grooming, as well as from training privately owned dogs, pays for the food, veterinary care, and other expenses of the dogs being trained as service dogs. The trained service dogs are given free to people who need them.

Dogs who enter the program but who do not pass the necessary tests to become service or therapy dogs are put up for adoption as Paroled Pets. They get basic obedience training and must pass the American Kennel Club's Good Citizen test, making them far more desirable as pets than when they entered the program.

The PPPP helps people, too. Prisoners who learn to groom or train dogs are in demand. Jeanne Hampl often gets calls from potential employers asking when the next inmate from the program will be released from prison, and offering that person a job.

Since that first meeting with Jeanne, Andrea had watched for any shelter dogs who seemed especially alert and friendly. Whenever she found one, she called Jeanne to tell her about it. Several of Andrea's "discoveries" had been accepted into the Prison Pet Partnership Program.

Andrea thought of the PPPP as she stood outside Bridgette's kennel, watching the dog look and listen. She knew that service dogs must also bond well with people; Bridgette wagged her tail eagerly at everyone who approached.

Jeanne had also told Andrea that a few dogs have a special ability: they are able to predict when someone is going to have a seizure. There is no way to train a dog to predict a seizure; the dog must have the talent naturally and be able to use it. Such a dog can be trained to alert the person about the impending seizure and to take action during the seizure, such as getting help, staying with the person, or fetching the telephone. On average, a seizure-alert dog can give twenty minutes' notice that a seizure is coming.

The average dog's nose contains two hundred twenty million smell-sensitive cells, compared to only five million in humans. That's why dogs are used by police to sniff out drugs, bombs, and fugitives. Seizure-alert dogs have an exceptionally keen sense of smell and are able to sense differences that most other dogs, and all humans, miss.

It was recognized that dogs can predict seizures when a few people noticed their dogs behaving strangely just prior to someone's seizure. Researchers believe that the dogs pick up subtle shifts in body odor and electromagnetic fields.

The PPPP trained the first seizure-alert dog in 1983. There are now six programs in the United States that train seizure-alert dogs, but requests for such dogs far outnumber the supply.

Most people who have seizures have epilepsy, a disease where the nerve cells of the brain occasionally miscommunicate. The person becomes unconscious, and his or her body twitches or jerks uncontrollably. Each seizure can last several minutes.

When people who have epilepsy have a seizure, they are often injured. They fall down, or their jerking arms or legs slam into a hard surface. If they can know ahead of time that a seizure is coming, they can get in a safe place, like a bed or sofa, and avoid injury.

As Andrea watched Bridgette, something—a hunch? a sixth sense?—made her wonder if perhaps this neglected and untrained dog might be one of those exceptional few dogs who can predict a seizure.

Andrea had Bridgette spayed and took her home.

She needed to find out if Bridgette would be easy to train, and she had to be sure that Bridgette would get along with other dogs and with children.

Two weeks later, Andrea called Jeanne Hampl. "I think I have a dog for you," she said. "Possibly even a seizure-alert dog."

Jeanne accepted Bridgette into the program, and Bridgette went off to prison to receive her training.

Jeanne saw how sensitive and alert Bridgette was. She also noticed that Bridgette was especially scent-oriented. Like Andrea, she wondered if this dog might possibly be one of the rare dogs who can predict seizures. One of the inmates at the prison, Sally (not her real name), has seizures, and she agreed to work as Bridgette's trainer.

Four days after Sally began Bridgette's training, Bridgette began to whine and nudge Sally's leg for no apparent reason. Because Sally had previously worked with seizure-alert dogs, she realized that Bridgette might be trying to warn her. Sally lay down, and a few minutes later she had a seizure. Without anyone showing Bridgette what to do, she had let Sally know that she was going to have a seizure!

In order to be certified as a service dog, Bridgette

needed one hundred twenty hours of supervised training. She learned both hand and voice signals for many commands, to respond on the leash or off, and to wear a service-dog pack.

Community volunteers took Bridgette to public places and home with them on weekends. Bridgette learned to lie still on the floor while a stranger stepped over her. She went to a shopping mall, where she was taught not to pay attention to children. In the food area, the trainer dropped french fries on the floor near her; Bridgette learned to ignore them.

Most important, Bridgette continued to alert Sally whenever she was about to have a seizure. Besides whining and pawing at her trainer, Bridgette barked in a different tone than she used at any other time.

After six months, Bridgette was ready to go to her permanent home.

Clifford Chartrand and his wife, Carol, both ex-Marines, live in Richland, Washington. Cliff had his first epileptic seizure at age twenty while he was still in the Marine Corps. After his discharge, he worked as assistant manager of a lumberyard, but the seizures became more frequent and more severe. For his own safety and the safety of others, he had to quit working.

When he was forty, a medication was found that helped prevent some of the seizures. But it did not prevent all of them, and he continues to have three or four seizures each month.

Cliff can never tell that he is about to have a seizure. Because of this, he cannot drive a car.

One evening, Cliff and Carol saw a television program about dogs who can predict seizures. Excited by the possibility, they called the National Epilepsy Foundation and asked where they could get such a dog.

The answer was good news and bad news. The good news was that one of the places that train seizure-alert dogs was right in Cliff's home state: the Prison Pet Partnership Program. The bad news was that PPPP already had a waiting list of people who wanted a seizure-alert dog. Because there is no way to specifically teach a dog to do this, there are fewer dogs available than there are people who need them.

Cliff and his doctor filled out the lengthy application form, and Cliff's name went on the PPPP waiting list. He had been waiting a year and a half when Bridgette finished her training with Sally.

That's when Cliff got a telephone call from Jeanne Hampl. "We may have a dog for you," she said.

Jeanne drove to Richland to visit the Chartrands at home. She wanted to be sure that they had a fenced yard for Bridgette and that Bridgette would receive good care.

Cliff and Carol had raised four children. While the kids were growing up, they had also had dogs and loved them.

Cliff and Carol are friendly, kind-hearted people; their four children and their seven grandchildren all live nearby. It was clear to Jeanne that Bridgette would be going into a happy and loving home, with plenty of attention and support from nearby family.

Before they brought Bridgette home, Cliff and Carol traveled to Gig Harbor where they met Sally, Bridgette's trainer. Cliff, Carol, and Jeanne were seated when Sally brought Bridgette into the room. Bridgette stopped and looked at the newcomers. Then she left Sally's side, walked directly to Cliff, and sat at his feet.

"It was as if she knew instinctively that Cliff was her person," Carol said.

Jeanne Hampl agreed, adding she had never seen a dog do that before.

The Chartrands spent three mornings learning the right way to work with a service dog. They learned what food Bridgette ate and how much. Cliff practiced giving the commands that Bridgette knew.

Cliff and Bridgette worked perfectly together from the start. Jeanne went with them on some trips to a doctor's office, a restaurant, and a shopping mall just in case they needed help, but they never did.

During the three days of instruction, Cliff did not have a seizure. There was no way to be certain that Bridgette would be able to sense a seizure coming for him, the way she had done for Sally.

When the training was complete, Bridgette went home with Cliff and Carol. While Sally was sad to see Bridgette leave, she liked Cliff and Carol, and she was proud of her part in helping Bridgette become a seizure-alert dog.

One Sunday afternoon, Cliff was sitting in his lounge chair reading the Sunday paper. Bridgette was napping on the floor at his feet, the way she usually does.

Suddenly, Bridgette woke up and crawled into Cliff's lap. She stuck her head up under the paper and put her muzzle right in Cliff's face. She licked his chin. She pawed at his chest.

"You silly dog. What's wrong with you?" Cliff said.

"Do you suppose..." Carol said.

Cliff tilted the chair back so that he would be lying down and unable to topple over sideways. Carol stayed close by.

A few minutes later, Cliff had an seizure. Bridgette had known it was coming, and she had figured out a way to tell him.

Thanksgiving came two weeks after that first episode, and Cliff and Carol went to their daughter's home for Thanksgiving dinner. Bridgette, of course, went along. She behaved perfectly until it was time to go home.

When Cliff and Carol started for their car, Bridgette refused to go with them. She ran around in circles, barking. When Cliff gave her the usual commands, she did not mind him. This kind of behavior is unheard of for a service dog.

The Chartrands thought Bridgette didn't want to go home because she had so enjoyed playing with all the children at the Thanksgiving celebration. They scolded her and put her in the car. Less than a block from their daughter's home, Cliff had a seizure.

"We know now," Cliff says, "that Bridgette was

trying to warn me not to get in the car. She wanted me to stay where I would be safe."

The first time Bridgette had alerted Cliff, she had done it quietly, by climbing in his lap, licking his face, and pawing at him. The second time, probably because she was in a strange place with other people present, and Cliff was walking, she barked and ran around. Because her behavior was so different the second time, the Chartrands didn't realize what she was trying to tell them.

Since then, Bridgette has alerted Cliff to an impending seizure many times. Usually she whines and paws at him. If he is alone, she also barks as a way to bring Carol or someone else into the room to help. It's a different bark than what she uses if someone knocks on the door.

If the seizure is a small one, Bridgette stays near Cliff, gently licking his face. If it is a major seizure, she gets far enough away that he can't accidentally hit or kick her when his body moves uncontrollably.

Due to other health problems, Cliff occasionally falls. When that happens, Bridgette runs to get the portable telephone. She picks it up in her teeth and carries it to Cliff so that he can call for help.

Four months after Bridgette went to live with Cliff, Jeanne Hampl returned to Richland. On this visit, she watched Cliff and Bridgette perform together all the tasks necessary for Bridgette to get her official service-dog certification.

A service-dog photo ID card—with pictures of both Cliff and Bridgette—is now carried in Bridgette's pack. If Cliff is ever questioned about Bridgette's purpose he can show her ID. This has happened several times. Once the security guard at a shopping mall didn't want to let Bridgette go in the mall; another time, a bus driver said Bridgette couldn't board the bus with Cliff.

When Bridgette has her service-dog pack on, she knows she is on duty. The bright red pack has a patch that says, "Please don't pet me. I'm working."

Cliff likes to take walks along the Columbia River, which flows near their home. Bridgette walks with him. As they stroll along the river, Bridgette is all business, her mind focused only on Cliff.

Sometimes Carol takes Bridgette for a walk along the river. On those occasions Bridgette does not wear her service-dog pack. "She's a different dog with me," Carol says. "She barks at the ducks. She wants to sniff other dogs, and chase after birds. She wags her tail at little kids. She does all the things most dogs do—but only when she is not working."

Since Bridgette joined the family, Cliff's seizures tend to be less severe than they used to be, and he has them less frequently. Owners of other seizure-alert dogs also report that they have had fewer seizures since their dogs have been living with them.

Jeanne Hampl believes this happens because knowing the dog will alert them ahead of time lowers the owners' stress level. Owners of seizure-alert dogs are also more confident about going out in public. If a dog starts alerting in a restaurant, for example, the owner can go quietly into the bathroom and lie down rather than having a seizure at the table.

Cliff agrees that the emotional security of knowing Bridgette will alert him in time for him to protect himself definitely makes him more relaxed. But he does not try to analyze what Bridgette does for him; he simply accepts it gratefully and loves her.

In a typical seizure, the unconscious person sleeps deeply for a time after the seizure stops and then gradually regains consciousness. Carol reports that when Cliff is coming out of a seizure, he now reaches for

Bridgette and strokes her fur, even before he is conscious.

For the first two years of her life, Bridgette had no name. One meaning of the word Bridgette is "lofty" or "noble." Surely, the name is fitting for Bridgette, the seizure-alert dog.

How to Help Shelter Dogs

If you love dogs and want to help those who need a home, here are some things you can do:

1. If you plan to get a dog, look for one at your local animal shelter. Some pet stores allow shelter volunteers to bring adoptable dogs to the store as a way to show them to the public.
2. Have your dogs spayed or neutered so they do not produce puppies. There are far more puppies born every year than there are loving homes to take them.
3. Call your local Humane Society or other shelter and ask if they need anything such as dog food, old blankets, or chew toys. Then collect these items or raise the money to buy them and donate them to the shelter.

About the Author and Her Dog

Peg Kehret has received many honors for her books for young people, including "children's choice" awards from fourteen states. She is the author of the popular titles *Earthquake Terror* and *The Volcano Disaster*. Her autobiography, *Small Steps: The Year I Got Polio*, won the Golden Kite Award from the Society of Children's Book Writers and Illustrators and the PEN Center USA West Award in Children's Literature.

Peg and her husband, Carl, live in a log house in Washington State. They have two grown children and four grandchildren.

They found their dog Daisy at the Humane Society when Daisy was six months old. Peg and Carl were working as volunteers that day, not looking for an animal to adopt.

Then they saw Daisy, and their hearts melted. The staff told them that Daisy was a Cairn terrier, the same as Toto in *The Wizard of Oz*. Peg and Carl, who already had a dog and a cat, agreed to go home and talk it over.

They never made it home. They sat in the Humane Society parking lot for a few minutes, then went back inside to sign the adoption papers. Daisy got spayed the next morning and went home with the Kehrets that afternoon. She is now chief squirrel watcher on their fenced ten acres of forest.

Every night at bedtime, Daisy gets in her basket and Peg sings her a doggie lullaby. It is a ritual they both love.

About the Photographer

Greg Farrar is from Seattle, Washington. His parents gave him his first camera when he was ten years old. He learned to use a darkroom in high school and took school yearbook photos. Then he went to the University of Washington, received a degree in communications, and started working for newspapers. About the same time he met Peg Kehret and began taking pictures of shelter dogs and cats for her monthly newspaper article about animals who needed new homes.

Greg now works for the *Issaquah Press*, a large weekly newspaper that is one hundred years old. He takes photographs for stories about current events, schools, sports, and interesting people.

Greg and his wife, Judi, live in Mountlake Terrace, Washington. They have three dogs and two cats, all adopted from animal shelters.